WITHDRAWN

09 JUN 2023

How To Build A City

TOM CHIVERS was born in London in 1983. A writer, editor and promoter, he is Director of Penned in the Margins, Co-Director of London Word Festival and Associate Editor of *Tears in the Fence*. He was Poet in Residence at The Bishopsgate Institute, London. A limited edition sequence entitled *The Terrors* was published by Nine Arches Press in 2009. *How To Build A City* is his first full collection.

Also by Tom Chivers

POETRY
The Terrors (Nine Arches Press, 2009)

EDITED VOLUMES
City State: New London Poetry (Penned in the Margins, 2009)
Generation Txt (Penned in the Margins, 2006)

How To Build A City

TOM CHIVERS

SALT

LONDON

PUBLISHED BY SALT PUBLISHING
Acre House, 11–15 William Road, London NW1 3ER, United Kingdom

© Tom Chivers, 2009, 2011

The right of Tom Chivers to be identified as the
author of this work has been asserted by him in accordance
with Section 77 of the Copyright, Designs and Patents Act 1988.

Salt Publishing 2009, 2011

Printed and bound in the United Kingdom by CPI Anthony Rowe

Typeset in Swift 9.5 / 13

ISBN 978 1 84471 564 0 hardback
ISBN 978 1 84471 884 9 paperback

1 3 5 7 9 8 6 4 2

In memory of my mother

Contents

Acknowledgements

Acknowledgements are due to the editors of the following publications, in which some of these poems, or earlier versions, have appeared: *The Alchemy of the Verb*, *Babylon Burning: 9/11 Five Years On*, *Charm Offensive*, *Dawntreader*, *Fire*, *Gists & Piths*, *Keystone*, *Nthposition*, *Trespass*, *The Wolf*.

'Queer Things in Egypt', 'The Coder' and 'Newborn' were commissioned by The Bishopsgate Institute. 'How To Build A City' was first published as a poster pull-out by *The Edgeless Shape*.

I am very grateful to those who have supported my work, in particular David Caddy, Anthony Joseph, Chris McCabe, Kira Milmo at The Bishopsgate Institute, Jonathan Ward, Tim Wells, Chris and Jen at Salt, and the Generation Txt poets. Thanks are also due to my family, my Dad and, above all, to Sarah Dustagheer.

Part I

Tube

A kind of lozenge, a pill. A kind
of bullet, ballistic-tipped to kill.
Cylindrical Tardis; horsebox, nave.
An altered telescope; a grave
(a kind of seaman's coffin).

An arch, multiplied: a trap.
A trick of lights and speed.
A fabric gunnel. The inside
of a sleeve. A sheaf rolled up
to swat a fly; a wave reversed;
a soundtracked sanctuary. A box.

This is yogic

She was found in a gully, Nordic features
and a beige ratatouille of sick in an arc.

This is yogic.   Anorak in the hedge
(*or henge*) and the piss tang of celeriac.

He was a Whitechapel rake and she,
well, no vestal virgin nor blood donor.

Ergo, the site of furtive bayonets
and paving the colour of wet tongue.

Talk is loose when the fog comes down;
archaic argots, hybrid whispering.

Dangling from a silo, the cunt with the
pink ukulele can hone his ego on my fist.

Citizen

They say the city needs this
realignment, a cleansing fire.

I stand ten feet tall, steak-fed.
A rolling mass submerges

into Autumn haze. Today
the Tube spews well-kempt

émigrés; pack-hunters breach
the wall, spill out the other side,

surprised to find it like this.
I watch my flaxen neighbour

stealing in, cradling his package,
a steaming pay-load of haddock.

I strut between the undressed stalls.
The market's quiet; just two kids

smoking, braced against the girders.
There is always need for linen

and cheeseburgers. Some say
the fire has come too late, the game

already up. But glass compels;
we never really see it as it is,

cannot get perspective. Kate Moss
on rollerskates. The grey tower,

still edging the sky; a ship
pranged, tailed and shaken

of its cargo. Watch the last one fall.
Unstop the leak, the glossy wound.

Brick by brick, unbuild the wall
and take a high position somewhere

south.   Frame another
panorama of the city, sparking flame.

Above the river, what looks like ticker-tape:
a billion notes airborne and alight.

Rush Hour

1.

It is hands that rush:
feet, fingers and eyes

before
one could speculate
but the way light is either
caught in or catching
smoke in the tunnel-dark

that it's there
at all

and we are just animals
but how he sat there
rational-looking and

that
makes you think

even an eardrum, burst, regenerates

there's something dirty
about words

now it's better to be silent

2.

Take me to the strand
and I will show you
the soft diplomacy of

rivers
      they do not need
            geometry

30 years on and we're here
again, cleaning body parts
off patterned upholstery

    3.

All the city's past
was here

a scrambling of
voices in the black
earth

we rose through
clay, salt deposits,
ammonites

    our digits
strained at marsh slip
and all the while
the world went on
through the pinhole
that was the bull's red
eye

a single silence masks
the creak and strain of steel
that was the quietening
of the thing itself,
that was the yielding
of the 'fruits of their

[8]

own choice':

72 virgins

52 bodies

4 bombers

1 god

   4.

Residual self-image states:
I enjoy double-espresso,
nuzzle in foam colloid
and do not concern myself
with the destination of shit.
I guess terror cells must be
like prison cells. I guess they
are equipped with toilet, basin
and bunk beds. I guess
they are like a monk's cell.
I guess there is much silence
and its occupants are hooded
or *hoodied* and tonsured.
But this is a free world
and I have choices to make:
how to hem, check, embank
and incarcerate water.

5.

Nothing has made me
more proud, so proud

I have seen
I have been

in the absence of any
other transportation

the first bomb went off
and the lights went out
and the square marked
area in the centre as if
the wiring was burning

I knew   we were told
as I walked   because I
could not bear   two views
                 of a short moment

Don't trip Larraine,
whatever you do don't trip

The call was registered
as reported   how   or how
they don't deserve   because
that is my routine and
I just didn't know you'll
be on your own and
into the footage

I was one

we had no idea if the rails

on the intercom
when I woke   and that is what
saved us all   when the
tunnel lights came on
and out of the end
towards the station
my heart
goes out

6.

This is the break of another day, the slew
and the still point. A rush hour of children.

The bull's red eye, his sopping undercarriage,
his burning smell up the walls of the tunnel,
between the carriages. The stink of sour gas
enough for you to trip in the dark before the
word is out. Are you as certain now? Was
that road there all this time, behind the glitz
of bars and trading floors?

The bull's red eye sees more than CCTV,
sees right through you, *into you.*

The bull *is* London.

Gang drones sharpen knives on his horns.
Currency traders stash winnings in his open
belly. The carriage doors clenched open.

7.

The ringing in my ears was the buzz of machinery.

The buzz of machinery became the sputter of lights.
The sputter of lights gave way to the strain of fabric.
The strain of fabric was the fall of footsteps.
The fall of footsteps was a nursery rhyme and
the nursery rhyme was a voice down the tunnel.

The voice was a prayer caught in the dust.
A prayer is a storm of sheet metal.
Sheet metal was the ringing in my ears.
The ringing in my ears was the buzz of machinery.
The ringing in my ears was the buzz of machinery.

Tina is a Rottweiler

I set the bathroom tap to run.
It stinks of soil; soil and turf,
coiled spiders in the pipes.

Fenchurch to Moorgate to Broadgate,
attire is navy blue, black, ash-grey;
display is a flash of pinstripe, weave, lining.

The tie is pure liquid jazz.

Other choices to make. At which
of three adjacent, similarly-priced
coffee shops to hold the investment
planning meeting.

I am soil, frappé sipper.

Tina is a Rottweiler. Her bum
fits snug in a black skirt.
Tina is synergy and results.
I am the spider in the pipes.

Seven Varieties of Knot

Beware slippage where the wall
disappears, distant legato
of phosphorescence. Two lines
meet here. I look across, see myself
surrounded by darkness, drifting
from one station to the next.

    [The reef knot]

Not quite a blood knot.
Moon-driven, stag-woman
caught in woods. Bloodhounds
froth, on tenterhooks, sidecar
                pans in.

Seventy plaques from Kensington
to Hyde to Green to James's, rich
with hay-fever and Bulimia Nervosa.

Pan may not drum his hooves here.

    [The figure-of-eight]

Bold as brass, the site triangulated
to a traffic island, bylaws' lung rot.
Too many uses for a tree. Hogarth's
Idle 'Prentice waits for the long-drop,
the thirteen coils behind his left ear.

John Austin was last to swing from
the 'three legged mare'; his corpse is
a shirt suspended from a rotary line.

[The slipknot
or hangman's knot]

First, open up the ends, revealing
each strand. A confluence of paving;
steps, a wall, then a garden. Rampant
squash overrun the vegetable plot.
Beetroot, cabbage, deadly nightshade.
Charmaine protects the tubers; she
weaves them six feet deep. A field splits.

Vaults, once overcrowded, house
shears, mower and gardening gloves.

Lean a headstone by the wall, just there.

[The shroud knot]

This is now perfect Vox Pop. St Nick
territory. There is no horse meat here.
Take up a sticking knife, a skinning knife,
a boning knife, steel, cleaver, bell scrapers,
meat saw, meat hooks. The diagram above
shows the principle of proper sticking.

Scald the head first while the hind legs
are dry. Then reverse the hog and place
the hook in the lower jaw and scald the
hind quarters. The heart is trimmed up,
washed and chilled. Leave the carcass,
a fretboard of cartilage. If marrow has

a smell, this is it. Loop twice, and to hell
with the cold caller. Gamble thee Swans.

And thus is it wholly bounded.

　　　[The cat's paw]

Ten tons of bus pulls in. Shish kebab
through the semi-transparency
of window. Acridity and loveliness
in perfect equilibrium. I could hug
a steaming cone of döner. I could.
Come off reeking of place at 3am.

Waiting at the request stop I was asked
for the time by a man with multiple
stab wounds and a nose full of claret.
I offered my handkerchief, but he
wouldn't have it. Landing so dark.

When you hear the sirens' wail
you run, just run, and the night
unravels like a Turk's Head knot.

[The Turk's Head knot]

Where seaside homilies find a home,
the moorings' echo, dank clods
of stormcloud beach a whale in the pool.

Lungful of salt
Noseful of salt
Headful of salt
Eyeful of salt

Palms fill with grit. Blueish, bilious
sands, torn blouse frontage, weathered
skulls of ruminant *Capra aegragus hircus*.

The British love tea and lashings of opium.
              Lungful of salt, burnt onion fumes.

No man is an island.
              Eyeful of salt, estuary run-off.

A river is like a rope.
              It bends, turns, knots.

        [The clove hitch]

Stopping Doctor Syntax

after Thos. Rowlandson

Stopping Doctor Syntax requires
a bung or a brace of long pistols.

Note the jawline of horse and rider
as they rear up, almost rampant

with unspoken vowels, consonants
and crunchy glottal stops. Too old

for Punch & Judy but that same chin,
that same grin, as in Losing His Way

or Pursued by a Bull or Loses his Wig
or Bound to a Tree by Highwaymen

or Visits a Boarding School for Young
Ladies. The stumbling schoolmaster

sees all. Black coat. Puff of white
horse-hair and a chin for escapades.

His good steed Grizzle, all skin and
bones, seems more human than he.

Georgian admen; origami of London
paving stones; John Bull's long-horned

topper; finally stopped with a stopper,
a plug and clot for his Taurean neck,

a flourish and fleck from his reed-pen
and then, the final Dance of Death.

Queer Things in Egypt

What 'Hang Theology' Rogers
began, this confluence

of people and purpose,
unwinds behind iron gates,

glass doors, green tiling
that screams Victoriana.

Open that door, there:
begin this rabbit hole tumbling;

internal architecture of pipes,
like a bathhouse inside out.

Goss, with pockets stuffed
with fivers, tracks down

ephemera, obscure literature,
shadows the maintenance staff.

There's a ceiling strung with lamps;
one lamp always swinging, pendular,

like untautened bootstraps,
exactly gauging the rhythm

of counter-culture. The domed
skylights sing with sudden rainfall.

Tell me this, Reverend: did you
find any queer things in Egypt?

The Coder

So, let's meet the coder.
He is the system architect.

You'll find him in an empty office,
debugging the backend.

He parses, line by line,
the grand façade, the face.

Bishopsgate glitches.
A fine mist rises, envelops

the building. Firewall: on.
The City accepts this new

configuration. He is pleased,
rocks back on his swivel chair,

hears a grumble of piping.
Sudden stink of earth, oysters.

The hard disc whirrs as
a programme loads up.

The coder smiles and clicks.
Cutout figures begin to stalk

imagined corridors,
form rows in a classroom.

Two cutouts assume
a common Yoga position.

In the Hall a faceless pianist
plays to a wedge of seating.

There is a knock at the door.
The coder stops, smiles briefly

and reaches down for
the Anti-Virus software.

Your Name Has Been Randomly Selected

Pennie Rakestraw emailed details of my order;
she claimed it helped performance in the bedroom.

Freuden Ginnery agreed and lodged himself between
the hard drive and the fan. He squeaks his sales pitch

on reboot. Morace Shakoor was kind enough to send me
excerpts from Victorian novels (he knows my taste),

cut up and reassembled as techno-futurist porno;
all tongue and motor, bonnets upturned in the mud.

I let the Trojan in. I'm nice like that. Besides,
I got the note from Hartshorne Settlemire,

installed the relevant import hooks and re-subscribed;
ham, bacon and eggs (my account is blocked)

converted to plain text by Waynick Quibodeaux,
who knows a thing or two about naming.

Big Skies over Docklands

High noon expectancy.

        Tower Hill
        Limehouse
Toytown Poplar
and the road crumples out of view.

From the train the water is not real,
does not move. The people, real enough.

Mudflats the colour of petrol.
Twenty years of stains on concrete.

The distant shimmer of a broker
as oddly familiar as a white man
in Cherokee territory.

Stilled cranes turned to public art
like the cradling arms of an angel.

    ≈

To journey here
is to listen and recant:
Mudchute, Crossharbour.

Herons Quay, reminding me of
home, the hunter,
locked away
in these names we use
to tie us to the land;
to this configuration of land
and water.

Our third city
awakens into steel
and pound.

The Trial of Margery

Margery, living at the Coppedhalle near the Herber in London, was
summoned for refusing to give up to Richard Coventre, clerk, the following
goods entrusted to her, viz. a locked chest containing a complete Corpus
Legis Canoni of the value of £10, a coverlet with a basin and ewer of the
value of 13s 4d and other goods worth 20s, and also a bundle containing
a box of deeds relating to the plaintiff's lands in co. Warwick, a basin and
ewer of the value of 6s 8d, a pitcher worth 2s, and two brass pans and one
of iron of the value of 4s.
— CALENDAR OF THE PLEA AND MEMORANDA
ROLLS OF THE CITY OF LONDON, 1381

Margery found no skulls
in the Walbrook.

In the Walbrook
she saw only pearls.

From marsh
an urgency
of water unfurls:
Dowgate,
Dowgate Hill,
the Herber. Inky black.

Imagine this: a freewoman,
no more than 30 on account
and of a spiritual disposition,
accused and tried for theft.

Of what?

The skin of a calf
taken, washed, dried,
stretched, bound and
scratched into new use:
to look in the eyes of God,

face to face, skull to skull,
and truly understand.

Margery saw pearls
swimming in the Walbrook,
the quality of light itself
sluiced in culverts
to make use and currency
in this new utopia
of copt or
coppered
rooves.

From the messuage
through the orchard
past the court-yard
and other tenements
the Walbrook rifts east
from west. She wakes
before dawn to watch
the bull rising from its
bed, the red of his eye
denoting the boiling of
blood as in a spasm or
sudden contraction.

When Pitt Rivers
reopened the stream
the skulls he found
were thought to be
the victims of Venedoti
fighters, mentioned by
Geoffrey of Monmouth

in the twelfth century,
spectral legionaries,
solid as ink or thought.

His workmen uncovered
round, smooth objects,
thought them pots,
giant eggs.

Piledrive this plot,
through Saxon,
Roman, preRoman.

Foundations must hold
against the barrage of estuary,
sewage outflow.

Foster and planners
in Walbrook Square,
empires of ice and glass,
in the parish of St John.

Margery looks on with a basin,
ewer and a box of deeds; her eyes
and ears are swimming with pearls.

Shaikh and the Fruit Pickle

Shaikh Muhammed Ali's fruit pickle
has a kick to stun even City boys to silence.
BlackBerrys left humming, deals up in the air,
and water, hurriedly, is ordered from the bar.

Pickle to strip enamel from teeth.

When Shaikh's father first came to England
it was different; Brick Lane was not for tourists
as it is now and you knew a good Muslim
when you saw one.

Once, working his family's land in Sylhet,
Shaikh dug right into a mass grave.

In the confusion of skull, kneecap and spine gristle,
they found three whole torsos—unspoiled,
still with skin and hair like the living.

It was said they were holy men, *hafiz*
who held the Qur'an in their hearts.

    ~

Shaikh, who makes the pickle we love,
put away his boyish grin
on the steps of Canary Wharf.

Her brothers came for him with knives,
to recover what was theirs by right.
He's not a Brahmin, not even close.

There was a tangle of limbs, shattered bronze,
where Shiva had fallen, alone, between lovers.

Invasion

Foxes are moving in.

The country is invading my city
as before, I, sou'westered, seraphic,
invaded National Trust properties
with my parents; hoarding photos
of deer parks and farm shops and
sculpted rusticity.

They leave beads of crap
on the lawn, gunging up
the mower. They bring forth
images of smoking cattle,
narrow lanes and land
in inimitable English Green;
not unlike the Lincoln Green
of Errol Flynn as Robin
in the tights of Victorian girls.

Tamer by the week, they slink
between the cars and houses,
knowing the alleyway behind
our house as well as I did when,
one balmy night, aged ten,
I walked its entire course dressed
as one of the Three Musketeers.

A Tourist's Guide to the East End

Wood becomes hammered after the public type: medium. London's truth fingers it. London is the foot of one, differentiated towards the east. For the city punishes the outside, the manufactured.

Question the person who causes the stone, voluntarily, to move. It may prohibit you from reaching out, to be with him. Compare him to the night, this donor of synchronization.

If estimated partly, the history of this restriction is like internment. Before the grain supported London, it coated a tradition. The tourist considers distant travel in his fingers. London presents the leg of a place, consequently an activity taken thus: the British, the ship, the war.

The way of the market is known. You offer ceramic good(s) and a toy. Leather materials are necessary. Processed field salad. The flow of motion. Sometimes dubbed 'slave of the east'—a road moving beyond. 400 independent shops. All that around the angle of one historic seat.

Hasty Excise

It all started in Europe's busiest railway station, a kind of troglodytic labyrinth: sixteen lines, no way out. You enter through a shopping arcade. Whitewashed corridors lead inside and then up. A vast runway of tracks and platforms, a boy in a blue tracksuit spitting at the rails and, beyond, the close menace of tower blocks. The speed is astonishing. Not the speed of the train, but the speed of forgetting. The streets below do not exist. Battersea, Nine Elms, Vauxhall are just the shitty verges of this eight-laned beast. I reach into London. Waterloo greets me with its velvet concourse, its has-been grandeur. The crowds, expecting my arrival, block the way.

Outside, the air is moist. It is 10pm. A fat baby gurgles from his pram. A skinny man in a grey suit sits with his back to the station wall, skinny legs drawn up to his face. He has no shirt and no shoes. The mother swerves to avoid a warm trickle of urine. There are so many people here. The heat brings them out. Below the footbridge, three obese tourists pose with Nelson Mandela's head as a disintegrating fireball of ash scuds along the concrete. I am moving so fast. In one ear, tinny samba. In the other, a raging chorus of violins. I am stereo.

The river has drawn back. Rest In Peace, Timo Baxter, skateboarder, thrown from the bridge when it was Hungerford, rusted, unlit, high tide. In the middle of the river, the stink of weed, an oil slick. I am moving so fast I almost miss her, poised, phone raised in right hand, head covered with a white lace scarf, on the point of speech. A boat passes below, heading east. The water disturbs. I am moving so fast, take the steps down two at a time.

This is another place.

Motion is a good name for a club. Young men in off-the-rack suits refuse to queue. Dark poppies appear on their white shirts. This is a bad place for a club. The sudden light of the Tube is like waking from a dream, or falling into one. Something gathers inside. I apologise. The woman is so large, I struggle to get by. I find a seat. We pass through Cannon Street without stopping. The lights are dimmed. The Israeli girl with the palest face and jet-black ringlets looks back at me in the window. When I stand up, I am taller than the man she is with. When we arrive and he struggles with a suitcase, I begin to hate him less. I am thinking about Zoroastrianism and the White Tower. I am thinking about how fast I am moving towards Aldgate. I am thinking about the man outside the hotel, his olive skin and pencil moustache, and what my chances are with the girls on the Minories, or the American who says as I am passing *it is brutal and sadistic* or the City boy crossing who says *win or lose, he's gonna get fucked* or the rude by the church who leans in as I lean back and in the alcove someone's sleeping, foetal, wrapped in white like a mummified corpse, a horseshoe of ham in grease paper.

I never expected the hole, an absence behind hoardings, diverted bus routes, a space for the sky, and I see now how things are made vertical. A renamed avenue. The empty car park. The butcher's hooks swinging in the wind. This light is like falling into a dream, or waking from a coma. I don't care what you think, this is landscape. Goulston Street falls away. The city spreads out to the north like an endless ocean and I'm just on the edge. Salt on my tongue, tonsils, lips.

I swerve to the right. Nobody is watching. Everyone is watching. Somewhere a casserole has been served. Somewhere unembarrassed laughter. My laptop boots up. The screen whitens. I am typing this now to make sure I forget.

Fifteen Days

I left you at Lewisham Station. You recommended
anger management websites. I suggested you fuck off.
This roundabout can't take the sheer level of bile.

File this episode away with the time you stole the key
to break in. You had the same look as that McCann girl,
beaming from another tabloid's anniversary cash-in.

Carmen, whom I later discovered was freelance,
manoeuvred me onto the spiral staircase. I clutched
a stack of hardbacks, withdrawn at random.

Drink? The wine arrived whilst I was sleeping.
When Ben approached, a chance encounter,
I was thinking of the climber, how it clogged

the trellis in Bishops Square. A sentence chugged.
My doppelganger is a middle-aged grunter in a blue
checked shirt with four young girls, one of whom speaks.

The leak still leaks. Their desktop basins are huge and shiny.
Your mother would have disapproved. Jude looked kind of
sheepish and her cheek, when I kissed it, was greasy.

Here's a list of things I might avoid the breaking of:
towel rails, walls, folders, us. Sebastian Tellier sings
No no no no no no no / Toi est moi, c'est comme tu sais.

The gay one from Shipwrecked is lost at sea. Mappa Mundi
as art installation impresses me, but you can't grasp
the lines, or how North Greenwich is a peninsular

and all buses go one of two directions. Upper middle-class
inflections drown out the talk of Trevor Eve. We leave
and as I clasp your hand, you whisper, *Really, I'm okay.*

How To Build A City

1.

Liverpool Street Station arrives flat-packed, instructions enclosed. At Point A, where the main escalator run-off intersects the natural left-right course of Essex commuters, cut along the dotted line between the confectionery and jewellery stalls until the departure board, the monitor at Platform 5 and the frontage of WH Smith are in perfect alignment.

Using the 5mm screws, enclosed, secure the taxi rank to the site of the Bethlehem Hospital, signalled by plaque. Open Flap C. This is denoted by a slight scuff on the paving towards the City, created by the errant trainer of an off-duty pizza delivery boy. This scar takes you home.

2.

Liverpool Street is gateway to the East. It is noticeably colder in winter than, say, Holborn or Battersea or Pinner. There is more mist at night and in the early morning. St Botolph's, 30 St Mary Axe and the half-erection of Bishopsgate Tower reach into darkness. The Station points somewhere. Another word for station is portal. Our eyes are drawn to a place with no contours.

To really go East—further than Spitalfields or Stratford or Bow—you have to go back. Back inside. The Station is a revolving door. But you don't want to stay in a hotel like this. Saturday night, The Wodin's Shades fills with alien accents. Colours conspicuous beneath polo shirts. Slip of nylon against hot flesh. Three meat wagons park up on Middlesex Street. Riot gear &c.

Many buses leave from here.

3.

Ponti's on Bishopsgate stays open all night. Purveyors of cheese-
burgers (£3, with chips) and assorted ciabatta constructions. The
time it takes the staff at Ponti's to deliver their famous cheese-
burger is roughly equivalent to the time needed to walk half-way
up New Street (adjacent), turn left into Rose Alley, deposit five
pints' worth on the back wall of the Police Station, and return.
These are approximate calculations and may require further
study.

4.

A porn bookshop, next to which: dry cleaners.

5.

Where the Station concourse gives way to the shopping plaza a
space is designated for regular displays of consumer products and
trials. In the past six months I have received:

1 Kit Kat
1 voucher for Paintballing in Surrey
1 voucher for Paintballing in Kent
2 keyrings
1 sample of deodorant

6.

Advice for Londoners regarding mushin

One morning, when you have nothing in particular to do, leave
your home and travel to the nearest railway terminus. Liverpool
Street is ideal but Euston, Kings Cross, Victoria or Paddington

will do. Buy an overpriced coffee; make use of the conveniently-located plastic seating; peruse a free newspaper. Discover a still-ness. You will find it truly liberating to exist without purpose or plan in a place designed specifically and meticulously for such things. To see the place not as the means to an end or in our tunnel vision way, but as a living, breathing thing. You may experience a state of Zen-like calm.

7.

On Middlesex Street two men in their forties sit up against the marble wall of a bank. Cells of orange light stretch to the sky. There is a wide streak, like piss, where their bodies have lain.

There are many buses, but none of them is going their way.

8.

If Bishopsgate is an artery and the Station the beating, bleed-ing fist of heart, and the buildings of the City all that sallow gelatinous fat encasing the heart, and the mess of alleys and cut-throughs the smaller vessels, all pumping, and when you look but don't quite see the van careering past the lights and can't quite turn to warn the woman who is crossing with her hair up on her head and as the blood in your eye begins to shoot and you catch the morning's headlines on the street vendor's board and someone calls out and something stops inside, can you be sure that it was your heart that skipped?

Sometimes I walk until my shins burn.

9.

Opposite the Station—the grey exterior of City Police HQ. At night its squat entrance spews crackheads, drunks and frauds onto Bishopsgate.

I always think policemen are taller than normal men. There are three possible explanations for this.

i. Policemen *are* taller. They are selected for their size.
ii. Policemen use their boots and headgear to gain a height advantage over heroin users and football hooligans.
iii. It's a case of perspective; my instinctive sense of a Policeman's authority causes him to appear taller than he really is.

This is how subliminal control of the mind begins.

Bankers are also known for their height and are constantly knocking their heads on the ceilings of their tiny sports cars.

10.

A golfing umbrella crosses the roadworks at London Wall. Waiting for the lights. Wading through the overflow. Crushing pasties underfoot.

Wading through the overflow. Turning at the railings. Out of the rain, following.

NO SKATEBOARDING
NO ROLLERSKATING
NO CYCLING

11.

We enter the realness of a place through metaphor. And then we speak it. The crack begins to form. It becomes a part of the architecture. All you need is a gap the size of a credit card. This shit is *charged*. This place, this name. That trick with a spinning globe and your index finger outstretched. And so the thread begins to unwind.

Knit me a home. Give it the ring of somewhere foreign. French-Norse riff on a Saxon bassline. Make the suffix *mean* something. Give me layers, strata, a geology of sound-sense in this wifipumped, cashsoaked, endoftheworld, alloftheworld, funhouse, partycapital, shitfaced, downandout, boomandbust, bendybus, redandwhite, sexy, straitlaced, licked, gelled and rolled, unreal, putative, embryonic, resonating city!

This is not Pinner. But there are many golfing umbrellas.

12.

I speak for Generation Y. We are post-viral. We were never 'off the radar'. Catch us if you can. YouTube campaigns are yesterday's news. Today an entire shopfront in Dray Walk is commandeered by the Mighty Boosh PR machine. Paradise of trucker hats. In Hoxton Square the windows of a sleek design agency are sold to the highest bidder. The streets are being branded. Naomi Klein's *No Logo* given the global fuck off gesture.

The tarmac is like Braille.

But Wren's Utopia failed.

From the Station a single decker bus follows the route of a submerged stream down to the Thames. Sat Nav or dowsing? Wait for the twinge.

At Moorgate I lust after a digital camera and trip over my heels where someone's placed a curb or a vista.

13.

It is exactly 5.28pm. The tube has stopped. The tunnel is half-lit where an intestine of wiring explodes out of the wall. I am gripping the overhead handrail like my life depends on the whiteness of my knuckles. I am possibly the shortest person in this carriage. The bankers are easy to spot but I speculate the remaining assembly must include at least seven off-duty policemen.

A thumbnail photograph of William Burroughs stares out from a poster. On closer inspection the poster is advertising an advertising agency. The snake devours its own head. I am back in the reptile house at San Diego Zoo.

14.

In Brick Lane youthful fashionistas espouse a kind of camped-up emo styling. Lo-fi forestry iconology meets regressive East Berlin electro. Butterfly stamps in endless dayglo reproduction on a classic black screen, a wall. They turn in prayer, genuflecting, to the East. There is little else to do. Pirate Wifi signals emit from their outstretched arms.

15.

Imagine the Thames Barrier fails.

No really, *imagine*.

We have made all this, all this stuff—to forget. To forget the city, this giant pan of settled land, wants to return. It wants to return to water. The city *wants* to flood.

Now imagine Liverpool Street under water. The Station must be twenty feet below ground level. A giant tank flush with river water; stairs and escalators turned to rapids of raw sewage. This is a video game scenario—disaster management for the Playstation generation. Press down B to hold your breath under-water and C to swim. Find the access key before it's too late! Pick up health packs from submerged shopfronts and the Tube as black as the centre of the earth.

I have never seen the river higher than I have this year.

16.

And I never realised flatcaps were so popular amongst the under 40s until I drank in The Griffin, Leonard Street. One pint of Flowers (IPA), one Grolsch, one Becks, one bowl of nuts (mixed). Avoid the pickled onions.

Crossing Great Eastern Street at the corner of Curtain Road, you find yourself triangulated by three East End estate agencies, each one trying to outdo the other. Foxtons; Stirling Ackroyd; City & Urban. When one buys a set of multi-coloured comfy chairs, another installs a light box.

17.

Today the sky opened up. In place of rain came coppers, five pence pieces, foreign currency. I looked up from the street to the row of second-floor windows, to the ones lit up orange against the evening. I searched my pockets for holes. The tinkle of cash on tarmac continued. Turning the corner into Middlesex Street, the night began in a landscape of impending stormclouds.

At 5.30 p.m. workers in long coats, umbrellas as weapons or beacons, stream from offices—Cripplegate, Leadenhall, Canada Square. This is dot time. By 6pm the City pubs are full. They pour onto the street. Bespoke pinstripes, Italian silk ties, impossibly sculpted.

Out of the City at Aldgate, through an acre of covered ground rapidly emptying of Porsches (Lexus for the family guys). Out, on foot, towards the East, towards the suburbs, and another place.

18.

I was too young for rave. I am too old for nu-rave. And I have taken to wearing leisure trousers at home, with elasticated waistband. I pad around the flat like a tiger, the city outside. I do not believe in irony, just multiple levels of recognition. A democratic onion, if you will.

The satirist looks inside. He satirises himself. The *brahmodya* competition ends in the silence of *brahman*. It's a kind of verbal flyting, a ritualised MC battle. The Owl wins. He is nocturnal. He fears death; not the Badger, snuffling the ground, a concrete sierra of city girdled by motorway. The towers are giant cedars, oaks, sycamores. A forest of moving ice. Everything returns to dust, like four floors of offices compacted into four feet of rubble.

19.

Olympic Breakfast at Ponti's. Talk of "theological space cadets".
These 9am egg and mushroom patrons! Business meetings over
bad coffee and worse service. The concourse moves below, a shift-
ing mirror. This futuristic throwback, London's double vision.

In New York, In New York . . .
In New York you can find Wifi on every corner.

I try to reimagine the Station as landscape—a rolling grassland
edged by cliffs. Rivulets, an ox-bow. This is liminal. Between
the wall and the limit. Whatever you want me to be. A Street, a
Borough, a Place, an Opening.

Log on at Fenchurch.
No fen. No church.

A fissure where the City ends leads right down. We build
up—impetuous. Perambulant texters on Brick Lane, outside the
Vibe Bar. A tangle of wires, rusted piping, forgotten sewerage,
every bit of owned earth; where the carriage lights shudder
between stops.

20.

Hoccleve walks, head down. Marlowe walks, from Norton Folgate,
lost liberty. Sinclair walks, from Hackney, past the Round Church
and pound shops. The 67 to Dalston is time travel. The Monster
Book of Trucks, ONE POUND. 35 unsharpened pencils, ONE
POUND. Bleach, unbranded, ONE POUND.

History is more than exposed brick or the looming, rusting arm
of a rig crane suspended above a Shoreditch house party. An
anonymous phone call at 2am. A moment coiled, held.

21.

"Fashion is, like / painting by numbers, yeah?"

Fractal vocabulary, the lingo of disintegration, postmodernity, underwrites a new singularity of place.

"The Creative Economy"
"The Shard of Glass"

Monuments to aspiration, an architecture of ideas and words. Inside the structure, it's like a sleeve, they say. It's like a fabric wave.

I almost enter a kind of false portico. New Street. Cock Hill. The sky clots. English Baroque, Kabbalic makeover. How To Build A City, from plans of a model. The Ring of Steel, London's Panoptican.

The snake devouring itself is really a dog sniffing its own arse-hole. The urban motif stamped on every wall, shop, bus stop and substation, in every underpass and locker, even in the salt scum frothing at the river bank, where the tide washes into gullies.

We are moving outwards, along linear paths, to an imagined future.

Part II

Snapshot

            Over the border
the taken, the missing, the dead
are ten years younger, in polo necks
and uncompromising 1980s hair, stare
goggle-eyed in booths for that snapshot
their wives or mothers will keep.

            At Metulla
the uncapped lens of a Sony Digicam
nuzzles in the heat of a day; they scan
the brown hills, the silent date fields:
"I came to take pictures, to smell it . . .
to see where the Katyusha burned."

Iconic

Sign language is iconic.
Polysemy is iconic.
Mark is iconic.

Iconic is the new ironic.
Aerosmith is iconic.

Louis Armstrong is iconic.
Neil Armstrong is iconic.
Psy-Harmonics is iconic.
Iconic is chronic.

Rocky is iconic.
The design of a Jeep is iconic.
The design of a Jeep is iconic
but crap just the way
Volkswagen is iconic but crap.
Smokey the Bear is iconic.

The nominal sign cap is iconic.
The jury's still out.

Yves Klein blue is iconic.
Bondi beach is iconic.
Kate Garraway in pantyhose is iconic.

The second system is iconic.
It is used for contour-tone languages.

Shatner the actor is iconic.
For Nimoy only the character is an icon.

The CIS Building, we agreed, is iconic.

Who is iconic?
The Beetle is iconic.
The vibrator! The rubber ducky!
Pride and Prejudice is iconic.
Santana is iconic.
Morrissey is iconic.

The resulting furniture is iconic.
Everyone agrees that this site is iconic.

The shot of Mario in mid-leap
into his schwanky new racer
against a plain white backdrop?

I mean that shit is iconic.

Marpha

And all was for an appil

Marpha, in the heat. Apples ripen
on trees in orchards, branches bow
from the sun with their heaviness,
lizards dart from the shade.

Apples are pressed into brandy,
baked into pies, left to dry
outside people's homes;
the local shops sell apples
freshly pulped into juice.

Marpha. The faint taste of apples
on sitting down to tea at midday,
our boots lying unlaced at the door.

Apples ripen in orchards
on postcards beneath mountains.
A rosebush urges at the window
as if seeing itself for the first time.

I am earthed by the scratching
of plump thorns on glass.

Newborn

Being but men, we walked into the trees
Afraid, letting our syllables be soft
For fear of waking the rooks,
For fear of coming
Noiselessly into a world of wings and cries.
                                    —DYLAN THOMAS

Birth is a kind of entrance. But how fast the river seems.
Faces turn to greet the moon. You walk into the trees.

Outside the rain collects in pools; a sudden breeze
runs through the Hall, and stops. You walk into the trees.

The city breathes, its pores secrete, it bleeds; streets
unfold, towers cleave. We open up and walk into the trees

and find a girl with knotted hair and matted, rough chemise
who sees herself reversed and flipped and tails into the trees.

The gates of Bedlam swing unhinged, release shale beads,
bracelets from the brickearth. All this turned into trees

will crease and freeze—nothing ceases but is stored, as seas
hold heat, as a heart grips another. We listen to the trees.

Refugees in borrowed clothes will come in twos and threes,
restock the valley, ford the rivers, walk among the trees,

map the perfect sphere of skull, still fusing, crumpled knees;
your eyes' dark blues and greens return a forest to its trees.

Being not machines but men, we misremember in degrees.
But then, as Thomas told, we dream and walk into the trees.

Guthlac

The year is 714:
holed up with the demons
of the reedbog my SOS
went AWOL in the fens
danced the Polka with ground-mist

Prophets of drainage
sluice and ditch
I am Guthlac

saint
hermit
so high and mighty they wrote me
a Vita and two long poems
in alliterative metre

The northern sky grows dark
I its swarthy accomplice desiccated
in the Welland's soupy depth

I am your past
your conscience
your desert fathers
alone out here like Bar of Sparty Lea
slumped at the Public's Convenience
with wag tongue lolling, rolling,
just pop-eyed Beccel for comfort—
willing slave
in my scooped-out spoon of cave
on my coughed-up gob of land
in my wilderness of bog

I Guthlac
time-rich, sodden
nothing to the man on the Circle Line
going round and round and round

I Guthlac
steadfast on my island
in my insularity
stamping at boundaries
lost contours of march
penned in the margins

transparent as
bone

cloud

God

The Voyages of Óttar and Wulfstan

Translated from the Anglo-Saxon

Óttar,
bereft of sextant,
draws by eye and moon;
leads his foamy craft,
his crew, from where the whale
is fifty ell in length, at least.

This place beyond
the Finn, this soupy
ocean.
            Óttar asks:
is it the land that bends
eastwards from the sea
or the sea itself that cuts
and scores the land.

My rigging is whale-hide!
My cargo: Biarmian tusks!

Óttar
notes the local taxes:
marten, reindeer, bear and seal.

No man-beasts
with heads in their bellies.

            〜

On Google Earth this land
makes pasta shapes in the delta
of Archangel, traction city,
iced-up railroad terminus.

The Finn
who dwell on the wild moor

where the land is small
have never heard of the Soviet.

≋

Wulfstan
under sail and moon
from Jutland's core
counts off names of
half-familiar places:
zones of influence,
power, ownership.

His ship is optimised
for speed and strength,
clinkerbuilt, the shallow
keel breaking in the slush.

It's like Rumsfeld said,
and these are the known
unknowns.

　　Watch
the Elbing deprive
the Vistula of her name,
before the fusing of the spit
enclosed the port.

　　Wulfstan
watches from the prow;
a tree in a field, an aerial mast,
the carcass of a man burning,
and another on a boat, frozen.

On Kinder Scout

All the skies are leased anyway
— BARRY MACSWEENEY, *Pearl*

We marvel how the peat bog got this high and black,
pause by the whitewashed trig point.
Bold wiry sheep sneak between boulders
where the wind is like a papercut or a slap in the face,
where I have lost all comfort of companionship,
where alliances wane, treaties wrench
under a few words' stony hairline fracture.

Consider loneliness: the absence of anything to say
but isn't it beautiful up here in the sidewinding rain
and isn't it time to turn back off the moor,
find a spot to camp. I hadn't gauged our selfishness.

Up here in cowberry, crowberry,
moonwort and asphodel
it's a fishbone in the throat
and I wish for pylons and concrete and railway tracks
where we are content with lines and with each other.

This language is not our own:
all the oxygen makes us mad.

Shatton, Kinder

My reading strategy is layered distraction,
    cross-hatching and doodles.
Newspaper reviews fill with biro marks.
    Baffled by 'Moorland revealing'
(stuck in bog, dry rivers of peat);
    the poem translates as
'juddering sign
    spreading upwards, / in the rind'.
Mandeville interrupts
    a history of Turkic expansion.

Looking up from the page,
sudden close-up of a horse through the fence,
the indescribable black eye;
its muscular jaw is a choke vacuum diagram.

    SHATTON
(scrawled caps on the grit-bin)

Neolithic signposts from space;
lukewarm tea and Eccles cake.
All night the bullfrogs croak.

We walked the veins of what seemed and felt like salt
for hours, *four hours*, or what felt like four, rough rhino horn
of route, you in a ragged t-shirt, until the hags closed in,
black banks of peat and slip we had to scale, knee-deep,
slick as oil, the reek of petrol crackling to the surface.

I turned to set the way; horizon,
or was it just the cloud-line, falling
by a boulder stack.

Upstairs, the land is as big as the sky.

Working in Stone

Adapted from Prehistoric Stone Circles *by Aubrey Burl (1979)*

Inside a bank that broke from the four entries, which are more like circles of rock, the damaged Cove interrupts an avenue. A field of thousands of half-completed stones visits him nightly. A stone macehead of striped gneiss meticulously deposited in line with the southern moonrise.

At Point B you come by a visible base of danger: a circle of symbols. No proverb. This profitable politeness of monument.[†]

You were always reminded of the entrance. Keeping old equipment. Radioactive table finds itself misleading. You determined the author, hockling between the extension and the left door. What follows is excessively new and there is need to increase the technical screening.

Five astroroofs coordinate sightlines to the interior. Before science, before it conceives and connects the human dedicatory. It shows the letter, the post, the proverb, the n.

One may walk around it. Superbly cupmarked recumbent. Only charcoal and decayed bones. Gaunt, grey and revised.

---

† Legends of witchcraft

Postmark Tullamore

I almost wrote you a letter.

You were kicking your heels
down the high street, Tullamore.

You were in Tullamore
drinking Tullamore Dew whisky.

It was summer; you
wrote nothing down.

This is the memory I didn't have.

You were in Tullamore
drinking Tullamore Dew whisky
at Molloy's, clay traces
on the hem of your skirt
and a dirty laugh the locals took to.

Resolute, in rain up Ard Erin,
in lichen and blanket bog,
lighting up by the car,
soaked through.

You let go so easily
we didn't have to wake you.

Photographs

I

There you are, backstage, in your element.
Chest falling out of a Restoration dress.
Brash as anything. A half-smoked cigarette
ready between fingers gently curled and
coiled like a child's. Mother, you were
not much more than one then.

> Someone's daubed a beauty spot to
> match the one you already have.

You revel in it, recall the time they
spotted you: a convent girl at the bus stop
on Arbury Road, dressed in a kaftan.
                    What a scene it was!

You always knew the drama doesn't end when
the lights go up and the curtains come down.

II

I cut me out to fit you in, your
left and downwards look electric
as the gold Fender on the wall
of the Hard Rock Café, London.

Elbows on the checkered table-cloth.
A half-smile not quite yet smirk, contained.
What you had to contain, *not say*,
                                    didn't need to be said.

And so instead there are photographs,
poems from photographs, choices to be made:
what to cut, what to leave intact.

You're looking down, out, past the frame,
where a blonde boy sits, still reeling,
with his shirt yanked up to hide his face.

Paramnesiac

I enter your name into Google.

You are not, to my knowledge,
a bell-ringer, landscape gardener
or Greenpeace activist; were never
any of these things.

Your lone true hit is two pages in.
A newsletter in PDF reports
the progress of the Liquidambar
and its 'stunning autumn colour'.

You are pre-web.

    This tree may still
outlive us all, you say, and I fall, am
falling, in the night. Behind my eyes
the bone-white screen is burning.

Thom, C and I

Reworkings of twenty-two diary entries
written by my mother in Italy, Summer 1991

1.

easily
hot, drugged sleep

2.

mill race and overhanging penthouses
immobile, hairpin
& I had escalope di marsala

Edwardian Death in Venice, people strolling
with dogs

Pan may not drum his hooves here

Thom, C & I.

lightning over hills, the lake

3.

gorge we drove our scruffy
Stations of the Cross and
another building colonized

models of Christ babtist by John the babtist

a photo of mum & dad by some steps
simpler and stranger than we had anticipated

as dusk fell   Madonna del Carmina
the town band

in memory his wife Isabella
the Botanical Gardens
built by a Scottish émigré

4.

sandwich along the banks
of the Arno metalled road
soon & were gravel (Montegiove)
then saw what looked like but was
in fact one big L-shaped room

wind came rushing in more remote
and strange   battered Zucchini and then
carved African statues, baronial hangings,
Indian artefacts, beaten copper, baskets
on his bedroom wall!

5.

E. extraordinary (varieties of blue, ordinary
German blue and the more expansive acqua
ultramarine from Lapis Lazuli)

Disquiet, Reflection, Iniquity, Submission,
Merit, the language of gesture, warm and safe

Thomas

so quiet
you can hear the woodworm in the beams

   6.

locked, very stern
and unornamented

a motley crowd with
much evidence
of inbreeding

unable to find the key

2 levels, with the animals'
byres below   gravity shower

byres   a kiln

to negotiate gingerly the ascent

   7.

the most impossible impenetrable
impossible topography   on several hills
a car park
through
medieval ruins the Corso
& the Town Hall

(mainly locked)

(sculpted)

(actually a mixture)

& veal for Thomas

my favourite was a series of miracles of St Bernard
by Perugino & others which had wonderful vignettes
of him curing people with ulcers, occasionally post
mortem when he was shown hovering on a little saucer
of cloud

wonderfully camp
in his stockings
at the bottom
little whips in their belts

shaking so much had to stop in Tavernelle for a drink

   8.

missed his Adoration of the Magi

on the way home veal, potatoes & salad

an owl and foxes barking at night

   9.

wing collars, T, C & I

Also old books, but all
the good ones in Italian

10.

at The Sanctuary as we had feared
a Mannerist temple covered all around
& nut-brown, wrinkled and referred
to us during the sermon which T. loved
& shady trees with mint & rosemary
picked around Greppo /

11.

sarcophagi, votive offerings & the red and black pottery,
also death masks we had to collect & drive there "subito"
and expansive tombs too many traces of red and black

Dark, velvety damp then a storm, foolishly Etruscan
quite terrifying van of nuns from inside & we drove
specialising in liver complaints doing time whom as the name
suggests we tailed up the street, beat the hell out of

but the most unexpected drama of the altarpiece by Taddeo di
    Bartolo
miraculously peaceful, solemn & blue & white

12.

150 times!

13.

but T. & E. by accident
to collect to see but inside
to buy to show us what we hadn't seen
with blood from the Host   very muscular
by much tampering from the Tavernelle Butcher

14.

Despite their best efforts
to make us dislike, it is
impossible to dislike
on foot
which seemed the proper way, long shorts
& a long-sleeved silk jacket   by guile
when his back was turned

his sandals, habit and signature

at least
in vain

in a dust storm

15.

to return to take us to
making lace in main street
who had travelled on the lake
which made us jump out of our seats

16.

but still hot about Love and Travel

17.

from Streatham! for 50,000
and the little racing circuit
with the ponies and cars

Armani etc.

says that
but no politician dares,
by calling after
their families

18.

no strawberries which is one-sided,
bitchy & we have been moved about
the one we had accidentally trespassed into
all for 2 Indians and chiselling tools

I was batman
as documented earlier by Thomas

19.

ruckus etc. back into
unlikely I think my fault
I said saying I couldn't
said that that just
trying it on
but which is
fortunate

20.

(£13.00)
dull rather morose
as 3 people
played Alpenhorns
E. got the giggles

some kind of accordion
sausage but no shops
near the border

21.

some astonishing
engineering about 5pm

22.

vibrating noises
& busker at 2.15pm

Lightning Source UK Ltd.
Milton Keynes UK
UKOW04f0621110915

258421UK00002B/69/P